D0832920

Summer with Monika

Poetry

It Never Rains

As Far As I Know

That Awkward Age

The Way Things Are

Everyday Eclipses

Collected Poems

Selected Poems

Penguin Modern Poets, 4 & 10

The Mersey Sound (with Adrian Henri and Brian Patten)

For Children

Poetry Pie

Sky in the Pie

Until I Met Dudley

Dotty Inventions

Bad, Bad Cats

Good Enough to Eat

The Bee's Knees

All the Best (selected poems)

Slapstick

An Imaginary Menagerie

Lucky

Theatre

Tartuffe

The Hypochondriac

The Misanthrope

Autobiography

Said and Done

Summer with Monika

Roger McGough

Illustrated by Chris Riddell

VIKING
an imprint of
PENGUIN BOOKS

VIKING

UK | USA | Canada | Ireland | Australia
India | New Zealand | South Africa

Viking is part of the Penguin Random House group of companies whose addresses can be found at global.penguinrandomhouse.com.

First published by Michael Joseph 1967
Reprinted with illustrations by Peter Blake by Whizzard Press in association with André Deutsch 1978
Published in Penguin Books 1990
This edition with illustrations by Chris Riddell published by Viking 2017
001

Set in 12.5/15.5 by ITC Bookman
Typeset by Jouve (UK), Milton Keynes
Printed in Great Britain by Clays Ltd, St Ives plc

A CIP catalogue record for this book is available from the British Library

ISBN: 978–0–241–29438–3

www.greenpenguin.co.uk

I.

THEY SAY THE SUN SHONE NOW AND AGAIN
BUT IT WAS GENERALLY CLOUDY
WITH FAR TOO MUCH RAIN

THEY SAY BABIES WERE BORN
MARRIED COUPLES MADE LOVE
(OFTEN WITH EACHOTHER)
AND PEOPLE DIED
(SOMETIMES VIOLENTLY)

FOR I LOCKED A YELLOWDOOR
AND I THREW AWAY THE KEY
AND I SPENT SUMMER WITH MONIKA
AND MONIKA SPENT SUMMER WITH ME

UNLIKE EVERYBODY ELSE
WE MADE FRIENDS WITH THE WEATHER...

MOSTDAYS THE SUN CALLED
                AND SPRAWLED
       ALLOVER THE PLACE
OR THE WIND BLEW IN,
       AS BREEZILY AS EVER
AND RAN ITS FINGERS THROUGH OUR HAIR

BUT USUALLY
IT WAS THE MOON THAT KEPT US COMPANY

SOMEDAYS WE THOUGHT ABOUT THE SEASIDE
AND BUILT SANDCASTLES ON THE BLANKETS
AND PADDLED IN THE PILLOWS

OR SWAM IN THE SINK
AND PLAYED WITH THE SHOALS OF DISHES

OTHERDAYS WE WENT FOR LONG WALKS
AROUND THE TABLE
AND PICNICKED ON THE BANKS
OF THE SETTEE

OR JUST SUNBATHED LAZILY
IN FRONT OF THE FIRE

UNTIL THE SHILLING SET ON THE HORIZON

WE DANCED A LOT THAT SUMMER...
BOSSANOVAED BY THE BOOKCASE
OR MADISONED INSTEAD
HULLIGULLIED BY THE OVEN
OR TWISTED ROUND THE BED

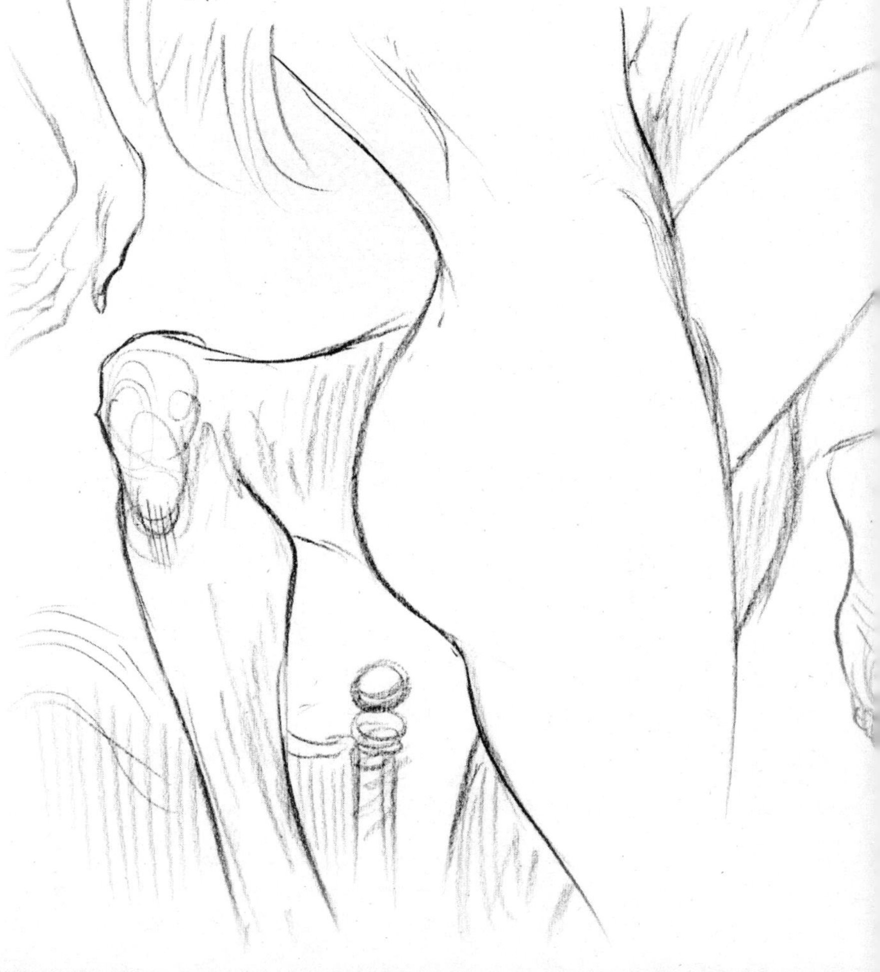

AT FIRST WE KEPT BIRDS
  IN A TRANSISTOR BOX
  TO SING FOR US
  BUT SADLY THEY DIED
WE BEING TOO EMBRACED IN EACHOTHER
      TO FEED THEM

BUT IT DIDN'T REALLY MATTER
BECAUSE WE MADE LOVESONGS WITH OUR BODIES
I BECAME THE WORDS
AND SHE PUT ME TO MUSIC

THEY SAY IT WAS JUST
          LIKE
        ANYOTHER
          SUMMER

... BUT IT WASN'T

FOR WE HAD LOVE AND EACHOTHER
AND THE MOON FOR COMPANY
WHEN I SPENT SUMMER WITH MONIKA
    AND   MONIKA
        SPENT SUMMER

              WITHME

TEN MILK BOTTLES STANDING IN THE HALL
TEN MILK BOTTLES UP AGAINST THE WALL
NEXT DOOR NEIGHBOUR THINKS WE'RE DEAD
HASN'T HEARD A SOUND HE SAID
DOESN'T KNOW WE'VE BEEN IN BED
THE TEN WHOLE DAYS SINCE WE WERE WED

NO ONE KNOWS AND NO ONE SEES
WE LOVERS DOING AS WE PLEASE

BUT PEOPLE STOP AND POINT AT THESE
TEN MILK BOTTLES A-TURNING INTO CHEESE

TEN MILK BOTTLES STANDING DAY AND NIGHT
TEN DIFFERENT THICKNESSES AND
DIFFERENT SHADES OF WHITE
PERSISTENT CAROLSINGERS WITHOUT A NOTE TO UTTER
SILENT CAROLSINGERS A-TURNING INTO BUTTER

NOW SHE'S RUN OUT OF PASSION
AND THERE'S NOT MUCH LEFT IN ME
SO MAYBE WE'LL GET UP
AND MAKE A CUP OF TEA
THEN PEOPLE CAN STOP WONDERING
WHAT THEY'RE WAITING FOR

THOSE TEN MILK BOTTLES A-QUEUING AT OUR DOOR
THOSE TEN MILK BOTTLES A-QUEUING AT OUR DOOR

3.

SATURDAY MORNING
TIME FOR STRETCHING
AND YAWNING
THE LANGUID
HEAVY LIDDED
LOVE MAKING

THE SMILE
THE KISS
THE "WHO DO YOU LOVE?"

AND THEN THE WEEKLY
CONFIDENCE TRICK:

THE YOURSAYING IT'S MY
TURN TO MAKE THE TEA
AND THE MY GETTING OUT
OF BED AND MAKING IT

4.

OUR LOVE WILL BE AN EPIC FILM
WITH DANCING SONGS AND LAUGHTER
THE KIND IN WHICH THE LOVERS MEET
AND LIVE HAPPY EVERAFTER

OUR LOVE WILL BE A FAMOUS PLAY
WITH LOTS OF BEDROOM SCENES
YOU ARE TWENTY-TWO YOU ARE MONIKA
AND ONLY WE KNOW WHAT THAT MEANS

WHEN THE MOON IS WAITING
FOR THE FIRST BUS HOME
AND BIRDS ASSEMBLE
FOR MORNING PRAYERS

IN THE TICKTOCK BLANKETNESS
OF OUR DUNLOPILLOLOVE

YOU OPEN YOUR SECRET DOOR

AND I TIPTOE IN

QUIETLY

FOR FEAR OF WAKING THE ALARMCLOCK

6.

I HAVE LATELY LEARNED TO SWIM
AND NOW FEEL MORE AT HOME
IN THE EBB AND FLOW OF YOUR SLIM
RHYTHMIC TIDE
THAN IN THE FULLYDRESSED
COULDNTCARELESS
RESTLESS WORLD OUTSIDE

7.

TAKE AHOLD OF MY MIND
AND GENTLY BUT FIRMLY
PUSH IT BETWEEN YOUR THIGHS

INTO THE WARM NUMBNESS
OF YOUR WOMB

AND THERE LET IT REMAIN
SAFE AND IN LOVE
WHILST YOU GO ABOUT THE HOUSE
DOING YOUR SWEET EVERYDAY THINGS

8.

THISTIME
LET THERE BE NO
GOODBYES
LETSSTILLBEFRIENDS
PARTING -
ISSUCHSICKLYSWEET-
SORROW

LET US HOLDHANDS
AND THINK NOT OF TOMORROW
BUT OF OUR DAILYSELVES

9.

MONIKA
I LOVE YOU MORE
THAN ALL MY REDLEATHER WAISTCOATS
AND I WILL NEVER GIVE YOU AWAY
TO THE NASTYMAN
WHO LIVES AT THE END OF THE ROAD

10.

IF I WERE A PARKKEEPER
I WOULD STROLLACROSS THE SUMMERLAWNS
OF YOUR MIND
AND WITH A POINTEDSTICK

COLLECT ALL THE MEMORIES
WHICH LIE ABOUT
LIKE EMPTY CIGARETTEPACKETS

AND IN A DISTANTCORNER
WHERE YOU COULD NOT SEE
I WOULD BURN THEM IN THE SHADE
OF YOUR LOVE FOR ME

II.

YOU SQUEEZE MY HAND AND
CRY A LITTLE
YOU CANNOT COMPREHEND THE
RAGGLETAGGLE OF LIVING
AND THINK IT UNFAIR THAT

DEATH

SHOULD BE THE ONLY ONE
WHO KNOWS WHAT HE'S DOING

13.

SOMETIMES AT DAWN YOU AWAKE
AND NAKED CREEP ACROSS OUR ORANGEROOM
AND DRAWING ASIDE
   OUR PRETTYYELLOW CURTAINS
GAZE AT THE NEATROOFED HORIZON
   OF OUR LITTLETOWN

WAITING FOR THE SUN
   SCREAMING WITH DULL PAIN
   TO RISE LIKE A SPARK
      FROM A CREMATORIUM CHIMNEY

THEN YOU PITTERPAD BACK TO BED
YOUR HEAD AFLAME WITH FEAR
YOU LIE IN MY ARMS
AND YOU LIE:

"I'M HAPPY HERE
SO HAPPY HERE"

14.

KNOCK KNOCK

SHHHHH....

DON'T OPEN IT
IT CAN ONLY BE...

THE ENEMY!!

SOMETHING'S GOT TO BE DONE
AND DONE RIGHT AWAY
MONIKA DON'T ARGUE
DO AS I SAY

I'VE PUT OUT THE MILKMAN
AND WOUND UP THE MAID
IT'S WELL AFTER MIDNIGHT
SO DON'T BE AFRAID

YES LEAVE THE LIGHT ON
THERES SO MUCH TO SEE
NOW MONIKA FETCH THE RAZORBLADE

AND LIE NEXT TO ME

16.

YOU ARE SO VERY BEAUTIFUL
I CANNOT HELP ADMIRING
YOUR EYES SO OFTEN SADNESSFUL
AND LIPS SO KISSINSPIRING

I THINK ABOUT MY BEING-IN-LOVE
AND TOUCH THE FLESH YOU WEAR SO WELL

I THINK ABOUT MY BEING-IN-LOVE

AND WISH YOU WERE AS WELL
                          AS WELL
AND WISH YOU WERE AS WELL

17.

I OFTEN HAVE THE FEELING
THAT WHEN TIDYING THE FLAT
YOU ARE NOT THINKING
  OF SHOES, NEWSPAPERS
  AND TRIVIA LIKE THAT
BUT OF A SKULLWHITE BUILDING
  WHERE ALL THE INMATES
  TALK POETRY TO SCRAMBLED EGGS
    AND WHISTLE AT OPERATINGTABLE LEGS
  A HOME FOR INCURABLE ROMANTICS
    A PLACE TO END MY DAYS

  YOU WILL SURELY HAVE ME COMMITTED

  I MUST RISE AND MEND MY WAYS

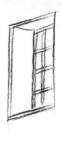

18.

AWAY FROM YOU
I FEEL A GREAT EMPTINESS
A GNAWING LONELINESS

WITH YOU
I GET THAT REASSURING FEELING
OF WANTING TO ESCAPE

19.

YOU DON'T SAY ANYTHING
BUT YOUR EYES TELL ME
THAT MY STANDING NAKED
TO SEDUCE THE MOON
AND MY CRYING BECAUSE
SHE WALKED RIGHT PAST
IS SADLY SYMPTOMATIC
OF A FATAL ATTACK OF
"PUSH YOUR ICY FINGERS
INTO MY BRAIN
IT'S SO HOT AND LONELY HERE"

20.

WHEN THE HADTOHAPPEN TIME CAME
AND YOU QUIT OUR HADBEENHAPPY BED
YOU PULLED THE BLANKETS O'ER MY HEAD
AND LEFT ME ON MY SADANDLONELY OWN

NOW I LISTEN DARKLY TO THE MEMORY OF YOUR
SMELL
AND WONDER WHEN THE SUN WILL MELT THE
STORM

OUR LOVE IS LIKE A KITTEN IN A WELL

THE DEATH OF SOMETHING YOUNG AND SOFTLYWARM
THE DEATH OF SOMETHING OF UNCERTAINFORM

21.

LAST SUNDAYMORNING
WHEN HOLYPICTURES
FLUTTERED
ON DUSTY CHURCH FLOORS
WHEN DOCKERS SNORED
AND MAMS WENT HEAVY
ON THE GRAVY BROWNING
YOU GOT OUT OF BED
AND PICKING UP A HATCHET
WHOSE NAME WAS
"ILOVEYOUBUTWECANTGO
ONLIKETHIS"

YOU MURDERED ME
BRUTIFULLY

THEN WITH MY TEARS
STILL SINGING
ON YOUR HANDS
YOU WENT TO YOUR MOTHER'S
FOR TELLY AND A LIEDOWN

YOU ARE A WOMAN OF MANY FACES
AND THE ONE THAT SUITS YOU BEST
      I FEAR
IS THE ONE YOU WEAR WHEN I'M NOT HERE
FOR WHEN YOU WEAR YOUR MARRIAGE FACE
BOREDOM LOUNGES ROUND THE PLACE

23.

YOU SHOULD NEVER HAVE SAID THAT
NOW
YOUR SMILES ARE WHITEELEPHANTS
AND YOUR FACE A PHOTOGRAPH
TO BE COMEACROSS
SOME SLOW BROWN SUNDAY

YOU SHOULD NEVER HAVE SAID THAT
YOUR TONGUE IS A MOTHER WITHOUT PITY
NOW
LOVE IS GONE
ANDANONYMOUS
LIKE THE DEATH OF A BIRD IN A CITY

24.

WE ENDURE COLD DAYS AND NIGHTS
OUT ON THE MOORS
THOUGH WE DON'T LIKE THE
COUNTRYSIDE AT ALL
BUT BY SPENDING ALL OUR TIME
OUT OF DOORS
WE DON'T HAVE TO SEE THE

WRITING ON THE WALL

MONIKA YOUR SOUP'S GETTING COLD
  IT'S CREAM OF CHICKEN TOO
WHY ARE YOU LOOKING AT ME LIKE THAT
  WHY HAVE YOUR LIPS TURNED BLUE?

WE SIMPLY CAN'T GO ON LIKE THIS
  FIGHTING TOOTH AND NAIL
WHY ARE YOU LOOKING AT ME LIKE THAT
  WHY HAS YOUR FACE GROWN PALE?

YOU'RE ENOUGH TO DRIVE A MAN INSANE
  GO COMPLETELY OFF HIS HEAD
WHY ARE YOU LOOKING AT ME LIKE THAT
WHY HAS YOUR DRESS GONE RED?

THE ONLY THING I'M SORRY ABOUT
IS THAT WE CAME TO BLOWS
WHY ARE YOU LOOKING AT ME LIKE THAT
HAVE I GOT CRUMBS ON MY NOSE?

ALRIGHT, I'M SORRY I HIT YOU SO HARD
BUT NEXTTIME DO AS YOU'RE TOLD
WHY ARE YOU LOOKING AT ME
LIKE THAT

MONIKA YOUR SOUP'S GETTING COLD

26

YOUR FINGER
SADLY
HAS A FAMILIAR RING
ABOUT IT

27.

WHERE HAVE THE SUNSHINE BREAKFASTS GONE?
ORANGE JUICE AND BACON
THE MORNING KISS AND TOOTHPASTESMILE
YOU SEEM TO HAVE FORSAKEN

NOW IT'S GREASY GRIMACES
EGGS FRIED STORMYSIDE UP
BURNT THREATS AND CURDLED ANGER

TEARS IN A DIRTY CUP

YOU HAVE GONE
YOU SAY FOREVER,
AND I HEAR NOTHING
BUT THE CLATTER OF OLD LEAVES ON STONE FLOORS

29.

THE SKY HAS NOTHING TO SAY
AND THE SCAFFOLDINGS ARE FULL OF DEAD BIRDS
THE MOON HAS PASSED AWAY
AND THE WIND HAS TEARS IN ITS EYES
NOW EVEN THE POLICEMEN HAVE GONE HOME

AND SCATTERED LIKE MEMORIES OLD AND WORN

THE LITTER
HAS

INHERITED

THE DAWN

SITTING ALONE
WITH MY BOTTLE OF SAUCE

KNOCK KNOCK

"WHO'S THERE?"

NOONE OF COURSE

31.

ONCE UPON A LOVE
WE SPENT OUR NIGHTS
BLOWING KISSES ACROSS
THE PILLOW

NOW WE SPEND THEM
THROWING PLATES ACROSS THE KITCHEN

32.

DON'T THINK I'M MOANING
OR TRYING TO PROTEST
BUT DO YOU REALLY NEED
ANOTHER NEW DRESS?

WHY NOT SMILE

IT'S CHEAPER AND JUST AS PRETTY

33.

... AND WHEN DEATH COMES IN
WITH HIS ZIP UNDONE

YOU'LL GIVE IN
AS YOU'VE ALWAYS DONE...

34.

LASTNIGHT
WAS YOUR NIGHT OUT
AND JUST BEFORE YOU WENT
YOU PUT YOUR SCOWLS
IN A TUMBLER
HALFFILLED WITH STERADENT

(SO THAT THEY'D KEEP NICE AND FRESH
FOR ME)

36.

I HAVE A WAR ON MY HANDS
EACH NIGHT I LIE AWAKE
AND SNIPE AT TERRORISTS
WHO RUN NAKED
THROUGH THE STEAMING JUNGLES
OF YOUR DREAMS

I AM ON YOUR SIDE
BUT YOU DON'T CARE
YOU ARE ASLEEP AND UNAWARE
OF MY FUTILE HEROICS
MY FEAR IS THAT ONE NIGHT
I MIGHT FALL ASLEEP
AND YOU WILL BE CAPTURED
MY SORROW IS THAT YOU WOULDN'T MIND

(WHY ELSE KEEP A WHITE FLAG UNDER THE PILLOW ?)

ONCE I PAID THE PIPER
AND CALLED THE TUNE
BUT ONE AFTERNOON
RETURNING HOME
EARLIER THAN USUAL
I FOUND YOU IN BED
WITH THE PIPER

YOU CALLED THE LAST WALTZ
AND NOW I DANCE SADLY
OUT OF YOUR LIFE

1 - 2 - 3

1 - 2 - 3

1 - 2 - 3

38.

I WANTED
MY CASTLE IN THE AIR
BUT IT VANISHED
WITHOUT TRACE "

I WANTED
MY PIE IN THE SKY
BUT YOU GAVE IT ME

IN THE FACE

MONIKA WHO'S BEEN EATING MY PORRIDGE
WHILE I'VE BEEN AWAY
MY QUAKER OATS ARE NEARLY GONE
WHAT HAVE YOU GOT TO SAY?

SOMEONE'S BEEN AT MY WHISKY
TAKEN THE JAGUAR KEYS
AND MONIKA, ANOTHER THING
WHOSE TROUSERS ARE THESE?

I LOVE AND TRUST YOU DARLING
CAN'T REALLY BELIEVE YOU'D FLIRT
BUT THERE'S A STRANGE MAN UNDER THE
TABLE

WEARING ONLY A SHIRT

THERE'S SOMEONE IN THE BATHROOM
SOMEONE BEHIND THE DOOR
THE HOUSE IS FULL OF NAKED MEN
MONIKA! DON'T YOU LOVE ME ANYMORE?

40.

MONIKA THE TEATHINGS ARE TAKING OVER!
THE CUPS ARE AS BIG AS BUBBLECARS
THEY THROTTLE ROUND THE ROOM

THE BISCUITS ARE HAVING A KNEES-UP
THEY'RE NECKING IN OUR BREADBIN

THE EGGSPOONS HAD OUR EGGS FOR BREAKFAST
THE SAUCEBOTTLE'S ASLEEP IN OUR BED

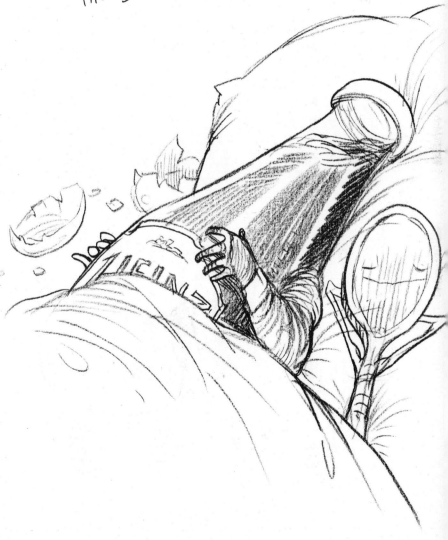

41.

IT ALL STARTED YESTERDAY EVENING
AS I WAS HELPING THE POTATOES
OFF WITH THEIR JACKETS
I HEARD YOU MAKING A DATE
WITH THE KETTLE
I DISTINCTLY
HEARD YOU MAKING A DATE
WITH THE KETTLE
MY KETTLE

THEN AT MIDNIGHT
IN THE HALFLIGHT
WHILE I WAS POLISHING THE
            BLUESPECKLES
   IN A FAMOUS SOAPPOWDER
I SAW YOU FONDLING
   THE FRYINGPAN
I DISTINCTLY
   SAW YOU FONDLING THE FRYINGPAN

   MY FRYING PAN

FINALLY AT MIDDAWN
IN THE HALFNIGHT
WHILE WAITING IN THE COOLSHADOWS
BENEATH THE SINK
I SAW YOU MAKINGLOVE
WITH THE GASCOOKER
I DISTINCTLY
SAW YOU MAKINGLOVE
WITH THE GASCOOKER
MY GASCOOKER

MY MISTAKE WAS TO LEAP UPON YOU CRYING

"MONIKA THINK OF THE SAUCERS!"

FOR NOW I'M ALONE
YOU HAVING LEFT ME FOR SOMEONE
WITH A BIGGER KITCHEN

42.

IN OCTOBER
  WHEN WINTER THE LODGER THE SOD
  CAME A-KNOCKING AT OUR DOOR
  I SET IN A STORE
  OF BISCUITS AND WHISKY
  YOU FILLED THE HOTWATERBOTTLE WITH TEARS
    AND WE WENT TO BED UNTIL
              SPRING

IN APRIL
  WE AROSE
WARM AND SMELLING OF MORNING
WE KISSED THE SLEEP FROM EACHOTHERS
                              EYES

AND WENT OUT INTO THE WORLD

AND NOW SUMMER'S HERE AGAIN
REGULAR AS THE RENTMAN
BUT OUR LIVES ARE NOW MORE ORDERED MORE ARRANGED
THE KISSING WILDLY CAREFREE TIMES
HAVE CHANGED

WE NOLONGER STROLL ALONG THE BEACHES OF THE BED
OR SNUGGLE IN THE LONGGRASS OF THE CARPETS
THE ROOM NOLONGER A WORLD FOR
MAKEBELIEVING IN
BUT A CEILING AND FOUR WALLS THAT ARE FOR
LIVING IN

WE NOLONGER EAT OUR DINNER HOLDING HANDS
OR NECK IN THE BACKSTALLS OF THE TELEVISION
THE ROOM NOLONGER A PLACE FOR
HIDEANDSEEKING IN
BUT A CONTAINER THAT WE USE FOR
EATANDSLEEPING IN

OUR LOVE HAS BECOME
AS COMFORTABLE

AS THE JEANS YOU LOUNGE ABOUT IN
AS MY OLD GREEN COAT
AS NECESSARY

AS THE CHANGE YOU GET FROM THE MILKMAN
FOR A FIVE POUND NOTE

OUR LOVE HAS BECOME
AS NICE
AS A CUP OF TEA IN BED
AS SIMPLE
AS SOMETHING THE BABY SAID

MONIKA

THE SKY IS BLUE
THE LEAVES ARE GREEN
THE BIRDS ARE SINGING
THE BELLS ARE RINGING
 FOR ME AND MY GAL
THE SUN'S AS BIG AS AN ICECREAM
                    FACTORY
AND THE CORN IS AS HIGH AS AN
                ELEPHANT'S

I COULD GO ON FOR HOURS ABOUT THE
                    BEAUTIFUL
WEATHER WE'RE HAVING BUT
                MONIKA

THEY DON'T
    MAKE SUMMERS
        LIKE THEY
            USED TO...

Letter to Monika

Dear Monika,

I know it's unlikely, but did you hear that *Summer with Monika* has recently been republished? If I had an address I would send you a copy as I'm sure you would love the new illustrations. Can it really be over fifty years since I last saw you? A lifetime.

In fact, it's so long ago that when people ask me what Liverpool was like in the sixties I say that it was like Hollywood-on-Mersey, with music and dancing in the streets, the sun shining every day, and everybody getting stoned and being nice to each other. A joke of course, but the fifties were so dully retrospective and conformist that things could only get better. They did away with National Service for a start, just in time to save me from a fate worse than jankers, and that gift of two years really made a difference to young men of my generation. Would John, Paul, George and Ringo all serving in the King's Own Liverpool Light Infantry have got together one night in a nissen hut and formed the Beatles? I doubt it. Billy J. Kramer and the Royal Corps of Signals? The Swinging Khaki Trousers? Gerry and the Square-bashers? Suddenly there were alternatives – art colleges, universities, all available for working-class kids. A generation of teenagers with hope and energy and time on their hands, who didn't want to dress like their parents or listen to their kind of music. Was it the same in Sweden?

And do you know what else they ask? They say, Monika, was she a hippy? Can you believe that? When Flower Power drifted across the Atlantic from California in the late sixties, many young people grasped the ideals of freedom and gentleness that it seemed to enshrine, but I was old enough to be cynical. What may have begun as a peace movement initially, an antidote to the horrors of Vietnam, had become a fashion show. It was fun, but essentially mindless. If I sound slightly jaundiced, it's not because I have jaundice, or because I believe that as a decade it is often misconceived, so powerful are the images of the period, but rather that it spawned a false sense of nostalgia that passed into the tribal consciousness of young people. They inherited, many of them, a sense of loss, an 'if only I'd been there' sort of yearning. What was exciting about the sixties for me was that I was young, and there's never a better time to be young than when you're young. The summer I wrote about was early sixties, pre-pill, pre-psychedelia, CND not LSD. As for the Permissive Society, it may have sashayed on to Merseyside years later, but if it ever went to parties, then it arrived just after I had left.

Decade

We never wore our kaftans or put flowers in our hair
Never made the hippy trail to San Francisco
Our Love-ins were a blushing, tame affair
Friday evenings at the local church-hall disco

Heard it on the grapevine about Carnaby Street
Looked for Lucy in the sky, danced to the Mersey Beat
There were protests on the streets and footprints on the moon
Times they were a changin', but the changin' came too soon

Those were the days my friend, there was something in the air
Though we never wore kaftans or put flowers in our hair.

Just across the road from the huge building site that was to become the Catholic cathedral was a former evangelical church called Hope Hall, and before it became a music and poetry venue, and long before it became the Everyman Theatre, it was a cinema. A sort of art house showing foreign films for intellectuals with a penchant for soft porn, and one evening as I was walking past on my way to the Philharmonic (the pub, that is, not the concert hall), I saw a poster advertising *Summer with Monika*, and I knew it was a foreign film straight away because they'd spelled Monica wrong. I also noticed that Ingmar Bergman had directed it, but what struck me most forcibly was the girl on the poster. Without clothes, you were simply beautiful, stretched out on the lake shore at the end of a golden summer's day. (There may have been a boy there too, but he has been erased and replaced with an idealized image of myself.) Monika, long-haired and naked, beside a lake in a pine forest. Very un-scouse. An image a million miles from Merseyside. Although I loved the poster and filched the title for my sequence of poems, I never did get to see the film, for which I'm thankful because it left me free to make up my own story. I led you out of the pine forest and brought you back to a tiny flat over-looking the Anglican cathedral where we went for long walks around the table and picnicked on the banks of the settee.

I hope you'll be pleased to hear that the poems were published by Michael Joseph in 1967. It was my first book and I was delighted. The trouble was that the publishers didn't have enough faith in the poems and twinned them with a short novel I'd written called *Frinck, a Life in the Day of*, about a young man who goes to London to seek fame and fortune as a singer/songwriter. This was early Scaffold days and some years later when we toured Sweden I thought of trying to find you and give you a copy of the book you helped inspire, but I was busy singing 'Tack sa Mycket' and you were … you were? I had no idea.

Monika managed to give Frinck the slip in 1978. In other words, a small publisher called

Whizzard Press published the poems on their own, with wonderful illustrations by Peter Blake, although the cover, a glorious painting of a girl sunbathing naked on a bed, was to prove too explicit for many High Street bookshops, who declined to put the books on their shelves. Despite this it sold well enough for Penguin to republish in 1990 (with a more chaste cover by Peter).

By the way, Monika, I assume you're familiar with Peter Blake because he's been world famous since he designed the sleeve for the Beatles' *Sergeant Pepper* album and was very much involved in designing the set for a production we did at the Lyric Studio in Hammersmith. Central to the design was a bedroom and Peter was keen to re-create the one from his original painting, which featured on the book and album cover. So while director Mel Smith was putting us through our paces in a rehearsal room above a pub in Chiswick, Peter spent the weeks painting tiny pink roses on to a backcloth to represent the wallpaper that extended on three sides around the set.

I would love to say that the show was a huge success and transferred to the West End before moving on to Broadway, followed by a round-the-world tour, which included a short season at the National Theatre in Stockholm where Ingmar Bergman, attracted by the title, dropped in and was so enthralled that he insisted on producing and directing the film for Hollywood (with you playing the lead, of course). But I can't. The theatre was packed every night and the audiences were enthusiastic. Unfortunately, the reviewer on the *Evening Standard* was less so; he put the knife in and that was that. The show never transferred. (Incidentally, Monika, the reviewer was not a butcher but a sort of drama critic. Do you have them also in Scandanavia?)

The show closed on Saturday 22 December and I spent until the unearthly hours with Peter and his favourite student, Ian Dury, drinking whisky in my flat on the Fulham Road. On Monday morning I went down to the theatre on King Street in Hammersmith to collect my things and clear the dressing room. It also occurred to me, and I'd mentioned to Peter on the previous morning, that a roll of his painstakingly hand-painted wallpaper might be nice as a keepsake. The thought of cutting the canvas backcloth into rectangles and having them framed, stored and sold over the years had of course never crossed my mind. But too late. On Sunday the backstage crew had dismantled the set and the delicate pink roses had disappeared beneath two coats of black paint.

And so, five decades later, I hold a little book of poems and I think about you and wonder whether you will ever read it. And I wonder too, what became of Monika, that beautiful girl, long-haired and naked, sitting beside a lake on a poster in Hope Street, Liverpool 8.

Love,
Roger